D0722773

J636.737 ST71
Stone, Lynn M.
Shetland sheepdogs

MID-CONTINENT PUBLIC LIBRARY
Blue Ridge Branch
9253 Blue Ridge Blvd.
Kansas City, MO 64138   **BR**

WITHDRAWN
FROM THE RECORDS OF THE
MID-CONTINENT PUBLIC LIBRARY

EYE TO EYE WITH DOGS

SHETLAND SHEEPDOGS

Lynn M. Stone

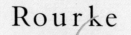

Rourke

Publishing LLC

Vero Beach, Florida 32964

MID-CONTINENT PUBLIC LIBRARY
Blue Ridge Branch
9253 Blue Ridge Blvd.
Kansas City, MO 64138 **BR**

MID-CONTINENT PUBLIC LIBRARY

3 0000 12876221 2

© 2007 Rourke Publishing LLC

All rights reserved. No part of this book may be reproduced or utilized in any form or by any means, electronic or mechanical including photocopying, recording, or by any information storage and retrieval system without permission in writing from the publisher.

www.rourkepublishing.com

PHOTO CREDITS: All photos © Lynn M. Stone

Editor: Robert Stengard-Olliges

Cover and page design by Nicola Stratford

Library of Congress Cataloging-in-Publication Data

Stone, Lynn M.
  Shetland sheepdogs / Lynn M. Stone.
     p. cm. -- (Eye to eye with dogs)
  Includes index.
  ISBN 1-60044-243-9 (hardcover)
  ISBN 978-1-60044-323-7 (paperback)
  1. Shetland sheepdog--Juvenile literature. I. Title. II. Series: Stone,
Lynn M. Eye to eye with dogs.
  SF429.S62S76 2007
  636.737--dc22
                                    2006010790

Printed in the USA

CG/CG

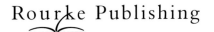

Rourke Publishing

www.rourkepublishing.com – sales@rourkepublishing.com
Post Office Box 3328, Vero Beach, FL 32964

Table of Contents

Bright-eyed and bushy-tailed, a Shetland sheepdog looks like a small collie.

The Shetland Sheepdog

The little Shetland sheepdog might be mistaken for a miniature rough collie, Lassie's **breed**. Indeed, Shetland sheepdogs (better known as Shelties) and the much larger rough collies share some common **ancestors**.

SHETLAND SHEEPDOG FACTS

Weight: 15 – 20 pounds
(7 – 9 kg)
Height: 13 – 16 inches
(33 – 41 cm)
Country of Origin:
Scotland (Great Britain)
Life Span: 13 – 14 years

Like the bigger collie breeds, Shelties began as working farm dogs. They herded farm animals on the rugged Shetland Islands of Scotland. They were good watchdogs, too.

Shelties depend on people to groom their long coats.

Shelties are good companions for people and for each other.

Today people love Shelties more for their companionship than their herding talents. They have become one of the most popular dog breeds in North America, Great Britain, and Japan.

The Dog for You?

For anyone attracted to the famous good looks of a big collie, the Sheltie is a downsized option. In fact, Shelties are in far more homes than the Lassie-type collie.

The collie is larger than the much more popular Sheltie.

Holding a "sit" is not a problem for a well-trained Sheltie.

Shelties make fine household companions. Shelties are extremely bright, friendly to their owners, and loyal. They are playful, quick to learn, and very willing to please their human friends. They do extremely well in **obedience** trials.

Agility courses offer a great outlet for a Sheltie's energy.

Shelties are too small to be protection, or guard, dogs. But they are quick to bark and they bark often, so they make excellent watchdogs.

Shelties are full of energy. They need planned exercise, such as a long walk, short jog, or a training session. Their long coats also need plenty of attention.

Many Shelties train on **agility courses**. There they can use their athletic abilities. They climb steps, balance, leap through hoops, and dodge through a row of poles.

Shetland Sheepdogs of the Past

Scottish herding dogs were the ancestors of the Shetland sheepdog. Some of these dogs were quite small, not much bigger than the Sheltie.

Farmers on the windswept Shetland Islands liked small, fast, collie-type dogs to guard and herd their ponies, sheep, and chickens. Those dogs led to today's Shelties.

A Sheltie, in merle coat, climbs a see-saw on an agility course.

While Shetland Islanders were developing a small collie, other **breeders** in Great Britain developed the large rough collie. By 1900, some Shetland dogs mixed with rough collies and smaller border collies.

Border collies are thought to be one of the Sheltie's ancestors.

Shelties are still at home in farm animal pastures.

In 1906, the first "Shetland collies" were shown as a pure breed. The American Kennel Club **registered** the first Sheltie in 1911.

Owners of big collies did not want the Shetland breed confused with their dogs. Collie owners helped force a name change to Shetland sheepdog in 1914.

Looks

Shelties are small, longer than they are tall, and covered by a long, straight, and somewhat rough outer coat. The long, outer fur creates a mane, especially among males. The undercoat is short and dense.

The Sheltie is longer than it is tall.

Shelties wear long, thick manes of hair.

Sheltie coats may be a mix of black and white, a shade of brown and white, or a mix of colors called blue merle.

The Sheltie's eyes are almond shaped. Its ears are erect, except the upper one-fourth, which tips forward.

Sheltie ear tips flip forward.

A Sheltie pup checks out a kitten.

A Note about Dogs

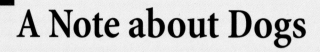

Puppies are cute and cuddly, but only after serious thought should anybody buy one. Puppies, after all, grow up. Remember: A dog will require more than love and patience. It will need healthy food, exercise, grooming, medical care, and a warm, safe place to live.

A dog can be your best friend, but you need to be its best friend, too.

Choosing what is the right breed for you requires homework. For more information about buying and owning a dog, contact the American Kennel Club or the Canadian Kennel Club.

Glossary

agility course (uh JIL uh tee KORSS) – a series of activities requiring athletic ability

ancestors (AN sess turz) – an animal that at some time in the past was part of the modern animal's family

breed (BREED) – a particular kind of domestic animal within a larger, closely related group, such as the English springer spaniel within the dog group

breeders (BREE durz) – those who keep adult dogs and raise their pups, especially those who do so regularly and with great care

obedience (oh BEE dee ents) – the willingness to obey; to follow direction or command

registered (REJ us sturd) – to have been listed on an official list or with an official club of that breed

Index

Further Reading

American Kennel Club. *The Complete Dog Book*. American Kennel Club, 2006.

Rayner, Matthew. *Dog*. Gareth Stevens Publishing, 2004.

Wilcox, Charlotte. *Shetland Sheepdog*. Capstone, 1999.

Website to Visit

American Kennel Club Shetland sheepdog page – http://www.akc.org/breeds/shetland_sheepdog/index.cfm

American Shetland Sheep Dog Association – http://www.assa.org

Canadian Kennel Club – http://www.ckc.ca

About the Author

Lynn M. Stone is the author of more than 400 children's books. He is a talented natural history photographer as well. Lynn, a former teacher, travels worldwide to photograph wildlife in its natural habitat.